JAMIEN MOREHOUSE
LIBERTY BANNERS

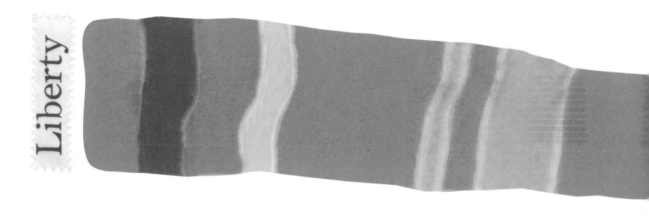

Liberty

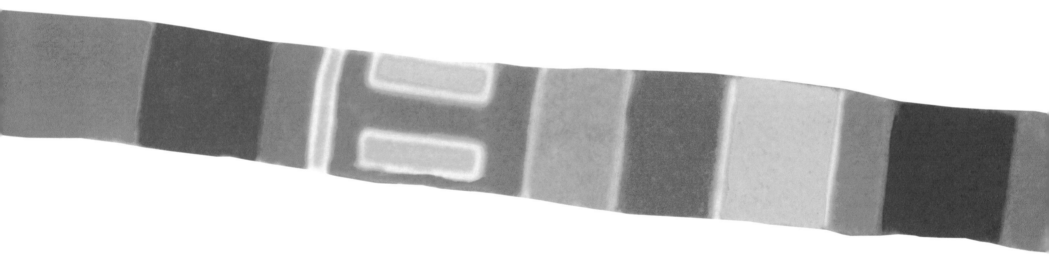

JAMIEN MOREHOUSE

LIBERTY BANNERS

FOREWORD BY

christopher crosman

ESSAYS BY

sam conkling

deborah sampson shinn

victoria k. woodhull

EDITED AND ORGANIZED BY

sam conkling

victoria k. woodhull

EXHIBITION ORGANIZED BY

helen ashton fisher

FARNSWORTH ART MUSEUM AND WYETH CENTER | ROCKLAND, MAINE

UNDERWRITTEN BY A FRIEND

Reflecting the artist's commitment to conservation and a greater environmental awareness, the pages of this book are printed on Monadnock Premium Papers, 100% post-consumer waste recycled paper stock and Process Chlorine-Free.

The typeface for this book is Bookman, a sturdy workhorse design for legible blocks of text. Designed by Ed Benguiat, this font was based on his 1975 revival of an 1860 design by Alexander Phemister for the Miller & Richard foundry in Scotland.

This book was published on the occasion of the exhibition *Jamien Morehouse: Liberty Banners* organized by the Farnsworth Art Museum and Wyeth Center, Rockland, Maine, on view from March 19 through June 18, 2006.

ISBN 0-918749-20-4
LIBRARY OF CONGRESS
NUMBER: 2005938742

PUBLICATION:
© Farnsworth Art Museum

ARTWORK:
© The Conkling/Morehouse
Family

PHOTOGRAPHY:
© respective photographers

© The authors for their text

ART DIRECTOR:
Sam Conkling

DESIGNER:
Harrah Lord, Yellow House
Studio, Rockport, Maine

COPY EDITOR:
Elizabeth IlgenFritz
South Montville, Maine

PRINTER:
J.S. McCarthy, Augusta, Maine

FRONTISPIECE:
Jamien Morehouse, 1978

For Jamien.

For Jannen.

Ladies' Home Journal Patterns

CONTENTS

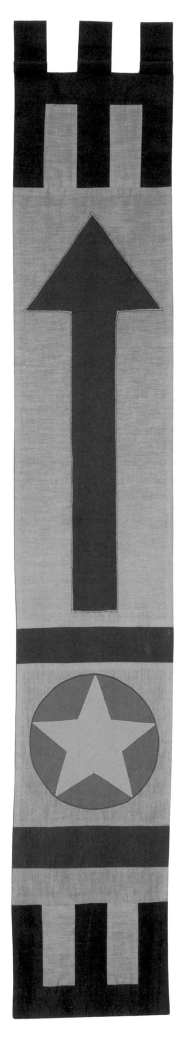

UNTITLED, 1978
COTTON AND POLYESTER FABRIC, 80 x 12 INCHES

FOREWORD

AS I WRITE ON THANKSGIVING EVE (2005), perhaps our most amiable and American of national holidays, I am reminded that Jamien Morehouse's legacy is far more than the visual record of her remarkable banners. Her artistic sensibility is inextricable from a personal philosophy that celebrated family, friendship and community. Banners, before they were emblems of authority and war, had been tribal insignias, rallying makers for like-minded citizens expressing communal messages coded to instill pride and inspiration and common bonds. So it is with Jamien's banners.

Jamien Morehouse's art emerged in the mid-1970s during the first manifestations of pointedly feminist art. Works by Eva Hess, Judy Chicago, Miriam Shapiro, Ree Morton and others began to explore themes, techniques and materials traditionally associated with women—pattern and decoration, sewing, domestic life and décor, ranging from the dinner table to fertility, sometimes all at once, as in Chicago's iconic *The Dinner Party* (1974–1979). At the same time, Jamien's earliest introduction to and inspiration for banners most likely came about as a result of her experience as a teacher in Poland (1973–1975) following graduation from Middlebury College. Eastern Europe, strongly influenced by the pre-World War I Russian avant-garde and with a long tradition of advanced graphic design, utilized banners and posters to convey not only political indoctrination but general communications among the masses to a degree most Westerners with access to a free press and electronic media would find anachronistic, if not quaint. In Communist Poland, banners and the allied art forms of the *affiche*—posters and broadsides—were ubiquitous and one of the few avenues of free expression and communication, ultimately leading to the Solidarity banners that heralded the end of communism in Eastern Europe. These banners, blunt and highly sophisticated in their seeming coarseness, are among the most powerful symbols of upheaval and change in the late 20th century. Morehouse undoubtedly learned in Poland that banners and graphic design could convey viscerally ideas and values in ways that are deeply personal, universal and immediate. Joy is Jamien's solidarity, her call to arms—in this case, loving arms, with a gentle, urgent message of utmost sincerity and seriousness that perhaps owes something to her acquaintance with the work of fellow Vinalhaven resident Robert Indiana, whose Love image is among the more highly charged images of American art.

On her return to the United States in 1975 from Poland, Jamien gravitated to childhood haunts on Penobscot Bay in Maine, where her family maintained a summer home on Vinalhaven Island. She briefly taught elementary school on North Haven Island, living in her family's rambling, drafty and unheated house and rowing to work in an open boat in brutal, frigid winter weather. During the late 1970s, Morehouse was the founding Director of the Children's Resource Center in Portland, the Director of the Maine Teachers Center in Rockport and also worked in the Environmental Education/Department of the Office of Energy Resources in Augusta. In late 1975, she established Liberty Banners, initially a sideline to teaching but which rapidly became a central part of a remarkably varied life dedicated to communication and learning at the grassroots level. When Hillary Clinton announced, "It takes a village," Jamien Morehouse had already put this precept into practice more than a decade earlier. In 1980, Jamien married forester, social and cultural environmentalist and founding director of the Island Institute, Philip Conkling. Kindred spirits, their marriage produced four sons, Tim, Sam, Micah and James, for whom the galleries in the Jamien Morehouse wing at the Farnsworth Museum are named.

Jamien Morehouse came of age during the 1960s and early 1970s, the crucible of late 20th century American culture when youthful idealism—not for the first time in the nation's history—began to challenge the culture and beliefs of the preceding generation. Ben Franklin would have recognized his own pragmatic idealism in Jamien's fierce resolve and ability to coalesce divergent viewpoints—conservative and liberal— around common aims. More so than most of her socially concerned, idealistic generation, Jamien was a builder who believed in the concrete expression of ideals—a product, most likely, of her upbringing and her father Richard's influence as a

successful architect of elegance and restraint as well as her mother Lee's pragmatic, moral and socially conscious nature.

Above all, Jamien's banners reflect a will to connect with the world, individual by individual. She invented an informal ceremony—the simple sharing of a pot of tea to celebrate the renewal of life and friendship—conducted at the spring solstice with a gathering of friends and, as the tradition spread through word of mouth, a vast extended family of participants who shared her beliefs. Through the enormous affection of those friends and in celebration of her extraordinary, giving life, that tea ceremony continues to grow each passing year as more and more people have come to realize that gentle civility is what binds us all. Certain traditions and constructs have ineffable meaning, especially when they encourage the exchange of ideas and feelings.

Jamien's banners were personalized for each

client but were infused with messages of universal import. Pigs appear frequently and refer to Greek mythology, symbols of good works and the Greek goddess Ariadne. Jamien designed wedding banners for friends that carried special, private meaning while conveying a sense of uplift and celebration. She once remarked that her love of banners had everything to do with how they "snapped in the wind." The wind—change and resilience—marks the moment. No one lived more in the moment or made us see those special, achingly beautiful moments more clearly than Jamien Morehouse.

Christopher Crosman
Director, Emeritus
Farnsworth Art Museum
and Chief Curator
Crystal Bridges Museum of American Art

PHOTOS (COLOR) OF BANNERS TAKEN BY JAMIEN DURING HER TRAVELS, 1973–1974.
JAMIEN IN WARSAW, POLAND, CIRCA 1974, FROM THE SCRAPBOOKS OF JAMIEN MOREHOUSE

ALL AMERICAN SHIRT, 1978
SEWN FABRIC SHIRT LABELS, 36½ x 25½ INCHES

BASTILLE DAY WEDDING, 1979
COTTON AND POLYESTER FABRIC, 123 x 55 INCHES

VEXILLUM

VEXILLOLOGY IS THE SCIENTIFIC STUDY of flags and related emblems. Concerned with the practice of flag design, usage and the theory of flag development, vexillology encompasses flags of all kinds, both modern and historical. Derived from the Latin *vexillum*, a term used by the Romans to refer to a kind of standard with fabric hung from a horizontal crossbar on a pole, it is the nearest equivalent in the classical languages to what we today call a flag.

Jamien Morehouse was both an accomplished artist and a vexillologist, one who makes flags. In her 24 years as a flag maker, 1975–1999, Morehouse created close to 200 singular works under the label of Liberty Banners. Her banners honor family, friends and ancestors; proclaim the celebration of marriage, birth and reunion; mourn death; hail welcomed guests; promote public and private business; advertise wine, fish, boats and a bountiful harvest; go to sea as ensign and pennant; communicate a subtle social comment; and enhance the swing sets of many elementary schools.

From inception to design, intellectually and physically, Jamien Morehouse embraced the tradition of flags and flag making. She was well versed in their history: In handwritten notes from workshops and speaking engagements she gave in the 1980s, Morehouse cites the lineage of Roman Crusades, the history of "Palio delle Contrade" parades of celebration in Sienna and outlines numerous anecdotes on the history of the making of American flags. Tellingly, her notes include historical accounts of hand-stitched flags constructed from foraged swatches of cloth, such as Jane Elliot making a flag from a red damask chair in 1780 and Captain Abrahams Swartout's wife stitching together a men's white shirt, a blue cloak and her own red petticoats in 1778. Morehouse also references in detail the construction of a ship's flag with white stars made from a wedding gown and a patriotic event in 1863 when the 16th regiment of Connecticut tore an American flag into pieces and placed these remnants in their pockets to save the flag from capture, only to quilt it back together at the end of the Civil War.

Morehouse's notes also tell of the making of her first flag when, as a child, she nailed pastel squares to a pole signifying that the older children in the neighborhood had hidden the Easter eggs and it was time for the little ones to hunt for them. During these same years, her own father called them all in from neighborhood play by waving colorful signs and banners of his own invention. Later, she describes seeing banners for the first time "in their finest and largest sense" in a visit to Warsaw in 1973. Upon her return from Poland, Morehouse began making flags of her own.

Cutting and sewing is a deliberate act. The making of banners and flags offers few opportunities for pictorial, artistic mishaps. There is no gesture of the pencil, no drip or splash from an overcharged paintbrush. While constructing her banners, Jamien Morehouse carefully and consciously placed form and color side by side, sewing them either by hand or with the help of an old portable Singer sewing machine. In her flags, looseness and gesture came in the way she acquired her materials. A champion of recycling, Morehouse used swatches of fabric cut from old clothes, curtains, tablecloths and many "good finds" at the local transfer station or flea market. She collected and recycled with a passion and found meaning in each and every item. She created her banners by manipulating the random textures as she found them, the colors as they came. While the chance findings of her materials led to deliberate and imaginative choices, she was a master at speaking through the predetermined pattern of found cloth, lace worn in previous generations, jars of buttons and boxes of shirt labels. A kindred spirit to her forebears' flags of petticoats and wedding dresses, Jamien Morehouse made her banners with what she had at hand.

Traditional flag making has unequivocal rules. For example, a medieval Guidon (a medium-sized flag of triangular shape) bore the affiliation badge (i.e., country) in the hoist (the part next to the staff) and the livery colors and personal badge of its owner on the fly (the end furthest from the staff). In essence, the placement of objects had a formula, the colors meaning. It is clear that Jamien Morehouse did not strictly adhere to the rules of flag making, however there is no doubt that she understood the power of the language. She was an artist who knew discourse of color, the power of symbol, the meaning of shape and the significance of the placement of each shape on the surface of the flags she constructed.

One of the first banners of the Liberty Banners Company was made for a reunion of friends at a pig roast in Vermont (*Fifth Annual Festival of Life, Close Enough, Vermont*, 1976). While the practicality of the pig roast dictated a silhouette, the pig as subject remained principal in her work for many years. The pig, a common domesticated animal, has long been a symbol of luck in numerous cultures, and dreaming of a pig, as indicated in *Ariadne, Sow of My Dreams* (circa 1976), traditionally denotes good fortune coming one's way. By placing these untraditional yet symbolic motifs—cows, pigs, fish, chickens, fruit and vegetables—within a highly traditional format,

Morehouse sends an almost subliminal message. What at first might appear to be mere gestures of whimsy are not wholly—the placement of these icons is deliberate.

The star, a traditional symbol that flags of many nations hold in common (it is also symbolic of the presence of spirit) and a symbol that remained in Morehouse's flags, often took a prominent role. It appears pictorially in Untitled (n.d.) and *Little Green Star* (1979), and in a more narrative sense in *Stars Above, Stars Below* (1978) and *Stars Above, Sea Below* (n.d.). In 1978 Jamien happened across a boxful of shirtmakers' labels and constructed *All American Shirt*, a gift for her father. Here, faintly reminiscent of the patchwork flag of the Connecticut 16th regiment, Wrangler and Arrow labels are quilted into a five-pointed star that carefully conceals a portrait of George Washington.

Historically, ecclesiastic banners included lions peacefully sleeping with lambs while serpents and dragons, which symbolize trouble, dominated medieval war flags. Morehouse knowingly replaces old icons of outward strength with those suggesting common uniformity, home, garden, and an overall reverence for earthly and celestial things. Her flags bear no dragons, no serpents, no American eagles. Instead she places the cow, a symbol of motherhood and nourishment, squarely between stripes in *All American Cow* (1982), she replaces traditional stars and stripes with a watermelon in *Liberty Melon* (n.d.) and she exalts the harvest in *Pears* (n.d.). Outwardly playful yet inwardly conscious of the language and power of all flags, Jamien Morehouse offers a new tradition to vexillology. She sends her message—

that there is always reason to celebrate—with a twinkle in her eye. By raising them up a flagpole, these ordinary symbols demand our respect and attention.

As a business, Liberty Banners accepted commissions. While Morehouse brought an air of the personal to all her work, commissions were admittedly not her favorite. Over the years, she created banners for capital ventures such as Great Eastern Mussel Farm (1986) and the Good Wooden Boats Company (n.d.) and a logo flag for Northcote Vineyards (1991), among others. Jamien made class reunion flags for Middlebury College, the alma mater she shared with both her parents, and her largest piece, *Landmarks* (1979) was a two-story tall banner celebrating Portland, Maine's historical architecture. In the late 1970s in five whimsical panels, she depicted a family portrait. In each of these works, Morehouse stitched the pictorial field with bold color and strong graphics. More unusual commissions included the design of a priest's stole and an altar banner for the Bangor Seminary in 1988, and an advertisement flag for an alternative healing center Joyful Noise in 1994. In the end, true to character, Morehouse's banner simply read "Joy."

Morehouse never really "made a living" from the income of her commissions, which is not surprising as receipt books show that she never charged much more than the price of her thread and a minimal amount for her time. Instead, each commission left a trail of personal correspondence, which makes it seem that each banner was more a gift between friends.

Despite the demands of making banners and a busy life on the somewhat secluded coast of

ARIADNE, SOW OF MY DREAMS, CIRCA 1976
COTTON AND POLYESTER FABRIC, 33 x 20 INCHES

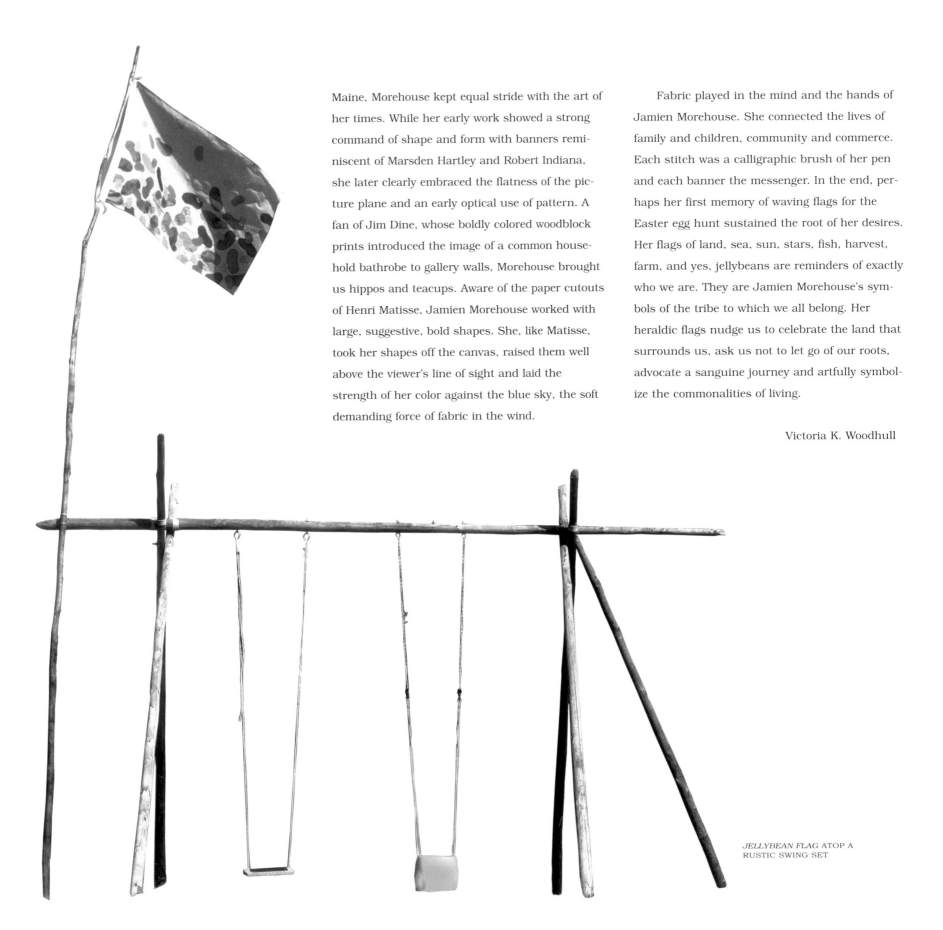

Maine, Morehouse kept equal stride with the art of her times. While her early work showed a strong command of shape and form with banners reminiscent of Marsden Hartley and Robert Indiana, she later clearly embraced the flatness of the picture plane and an early optical use of pattern. A fan of Jim Dine, whose boldly colored woodblock prints introduced the image of a common household bathrobe to gallery walls, Morehouse brought us hippos and teacups. Aware of the paper cutouts of Henri Matisse, Jamien Morehouse worked with large, suggestive, bold shapes. She, like Matisse, took her shapes off the canvas, raised them well above the viewer's line of sight and laid the strength of her color against the blue sky, the soft demanding force of fabric in the wind.

Fabric played in the mind and the hands of Jamien Morehouse. She connected the lives of family and children, community and commerce. Each stitch was a calligraphic brush of her pen and each banner the messenger. In the end, perhaps her first memory of waving flags for the Easter egg hunt sustained the root of her desires. Her flags of land, sea, sun, stars, fish, harvest, farm, and yes, jellybeans are reminders of exactly who we are. They are Jamien Morehouse's symbols of the tribe to which we all belong. Her heraldic flags nudge us to celebrate the land that surrounds us, ask us not to let go of our roots, advocate a sanguine journey and artfully symbolize the commonalities of living.

Victoria K. Woodhull

JELLYBEAN FLAG ATOP A RUSTIC SWING SET

18

FIFTH ANNUAL FESTIVAL OF LIFE,
CLOSE ENOUGH, VERMONT, 1976
COTTON AND POLYESTER
FABRIC, 40 x 36 INCHES

C.R.C.
1978

IF YOU ANNOUNCE THE PLAN OF YOUR arrival by telephone before taking the ferry out to Vinalhaven Island, and turn your eyes toward the captain's house on that last point of land before rounding into Carver's Harbor, you'll probably catch sight of a pair of figures stationed on a particular granite ledge over the harbor with raised beach wood poles, unfurling and waving furiously a dueling set of tri-colored banners by Jamien Morehouse, saluting your arrival.

With the sight of these two slices—in fact, brilliant wedges of melon, each trip to this place begins and ends, and so these banners are suited to mark an opening here, quintessentially Jamien, fundamentally graphic, strong in their simplicity, clever, and the slightest bit odd.

I started writing for this book in the attic of that captain's house on the third floor, once the ballroom in the days when the place existed as an inn called Rockaway. Up here in the room now a corner desk sits piled with materials beneath loose plaster of the dormered roof. From this lookout point, tacked to the walls around me, hanging from brass hooks in these bookshelves by my elbow, from pushpins pressed into this plaster ceiling, spread about on the surface of her now invisible desk is the work of my mother, artist Jamien Morehouse.

Beside the desk, a modest printing press, crate containers full to capacity stacked high, a mannequin or two, and leaning against the wall, the early portfolios of Jamien Morehouse detailing her work: etchings, banners, fish drawings, and assemblages built from gloves, stripes, castaway labels, and once missing buttons now repositioned by the schemes of exceptional design. They seem, most of them, born out of serendipity, created from the leads and fancies of intriguing moments, of being.

This floor was once Jamien's production facility. For two years in the 1970s, and virtually every summer when she'd return, the attic was her studio, and I remember it as locally famous for the scenes she directed here when I was growing up. She'd created some traditions for the space—I think it was Sunday nights especially, but people showed up at all hours, worked, left, continually came back. Jamien always had something going, some great idea pulling people in and turning creation out. A lot of her is still here, like a part of the worn landscape, rooted in.

On setting out early last summer with Victoria Woodhull to track down other pieces of her globally dispersed work, I found these things, banners mostly, some thirty years old, hanging on, maintained, flying in long honored places, usually faded, edges frayed by many winds, never unused. Like old souls, they hold forth still, with a particular, familiar, secure bit of energy.

Jamien's artwork was created with a belief in interconnectedness, and as we proceeded from her Kodachrome records or from leads penned into the margins of her notebook, Victoria and I could repeatedly find someone who knew someone who knew of the particular Liberty Banner we were after. There was a sense of a connecting thread of humanity tied to each synapse between here and there.

Jamien had both the eye and hand for stripping down message and purpose into single bold, essential, compelling icons. Her flags make their impression abruptly, color arranged against color readily understood for saluting a twenty-fifth reunion or advertising a fresh catch. While mostly uncomplicated in composition, twists of a subtle, sly humor of the unexpected hold forth in her collection. This is the direct wit that impelled the spontaneous conception of her legged fish and zippered *Blue Pig 1A* (circa 1978). A prime cut.

In 1978 Morehouse opened the Children's Resource Center where throwaway surplus too good to let go shelved up. Each thing, every affair, seems to have begged a new work in Jamien's mind, and functioned for her like the backwards acquisition of a tool for which the use would then be wrought. The Resource Center at her direction became the depot for spent tickets, odd plastics and a particular drum barrel I remember filled up with double printed poker chips direct from that one misfiring machine in Las Vegas. Jamien would drive off in an empty truck and come back with a delivery and fresh purpose, drawing together chance parts in new thought. She would have sixty collections going simultaneously, sixty marvelous groupings salted away. Baking soda tins, pins, buttons, Polish posters—a fascination in the consideration of each as a part of a whole, and a visual logic manifesting that ideal of interconnection.

Time is built into her art, each work factors a complete thought, a moment. And there's hardly a Morehouse piece without a back story, without a history, without an odd previous life culled from the embedded energies of its used parts—old documents, linen flour bags, thread, labels from abandoned shirt factories. It's as if Jamien found some moral imperative to keep and redirect the castoffs—for diminishing the waste stream while honoring too those lost parts and gone days. That subsurface spirit is consistent throughout her

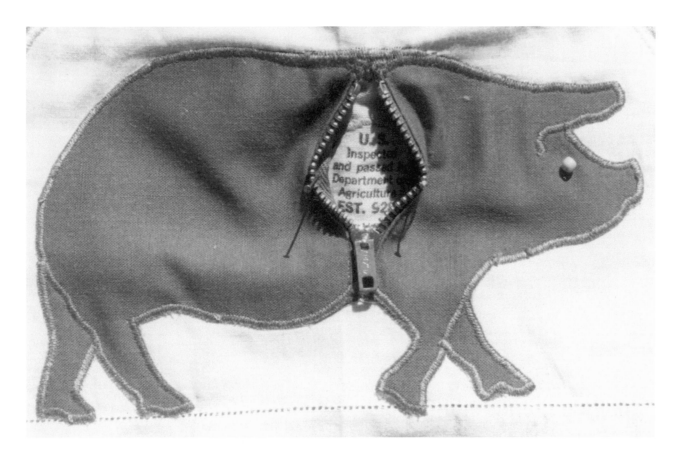

BLUE PIG 1A, CIRCA 1978 (DETAIL)

work—something there relates back to points in time with an almost audible articulation of its own genesis. It speaks in a language of exaltation.

Jamien's use of recycled materials and castoffs was the result of a vision tuned to the recognition of the miraculous. She was keenly aware that ordinary objects, these things we can hold or behold are, like the body itself, part of a cosmic system, like from Rockaway, where on the granite shore you can stand and sense the slightest curve of the ocean dipping into the far horizon.

When gathering this collection together last summer, collecting binders of those old Kodachromes, I hit pages and pages of what amounted to simple, extensive records of old signs, hanging laundry, revolutionary posters, open for business flags above the quick lunch stands off some town's dirt roads. These images must in some way mark a direction for Jamien's art, especially for Liberty Banners, for recognition of this rather miraculous interconnected system of comings and goings, roadside stands, the Big Men's Stout Shop, sizes to 70, Lane's Island, fresh fish. Movement.

Even on a calm day the banners don't hang flat, but fold and shift. From the intricate construction and consideration my mom gave to the joining of layer on layer, nylon to canvas, canvas to grommet, it is clear that she considered her work incomplete until the moment it's taken by its elemental final medium. And then when those winds are high, the messages double up, reverse, and beat to the lines of airstreams blown in from some storm, from some long off place—alive in the wind.

Sam Conkling

CYRK, 1964 POSTER
BY POLISH ARTIST HUBERT HILSCHER (1924–1999)

TAPS, 1986, NYLON, 52 x 94 INCHES

   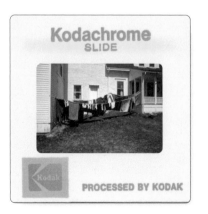

26

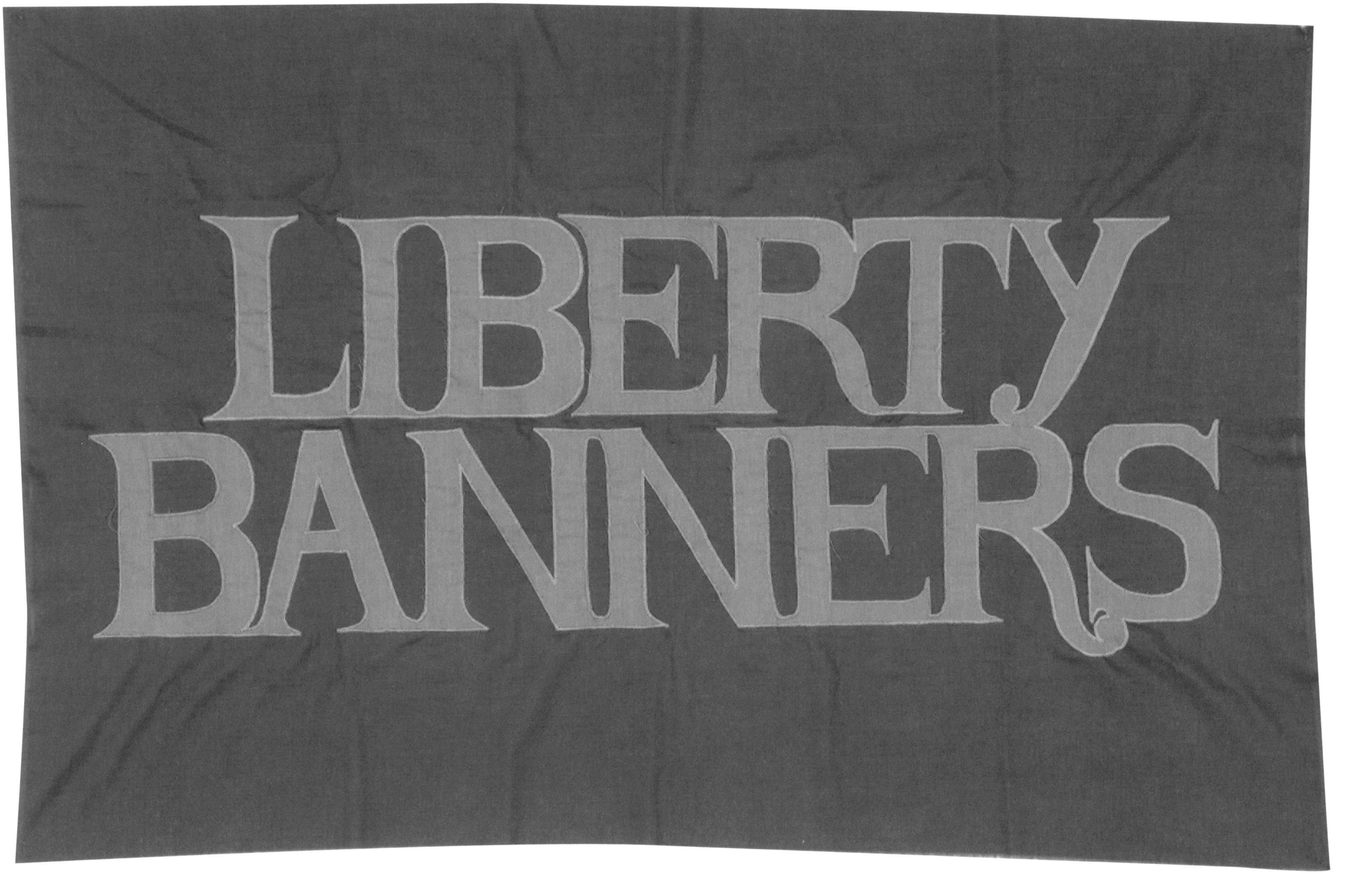
LIBERTY
BANNERS

CLAUDIA, 1976 , COTTON, LACE AND MISCELLANEOUS FABRIC, APPROX. 20 x 24 INCHES

EMMA'S CASTLE, N.D., COTTON, LACE AND MISCELLANEOUS FABRIC, APPROX. 29 x 20 INCHES

BLUE PIG 1A, CIRCA 1978
COTTON, LACE AND
MISCELLANEOUS FABRIC,
APPROX. 20 x 16 INCHES

SIXTH PRIZE PIG, 1976, COTTON AND POLYESTER FABRIC, 15 x 17 INCHES

CYRK. CURIOUS GEORGE. 1968. POSTER BY WIKTOR GORKA (1922–2004)

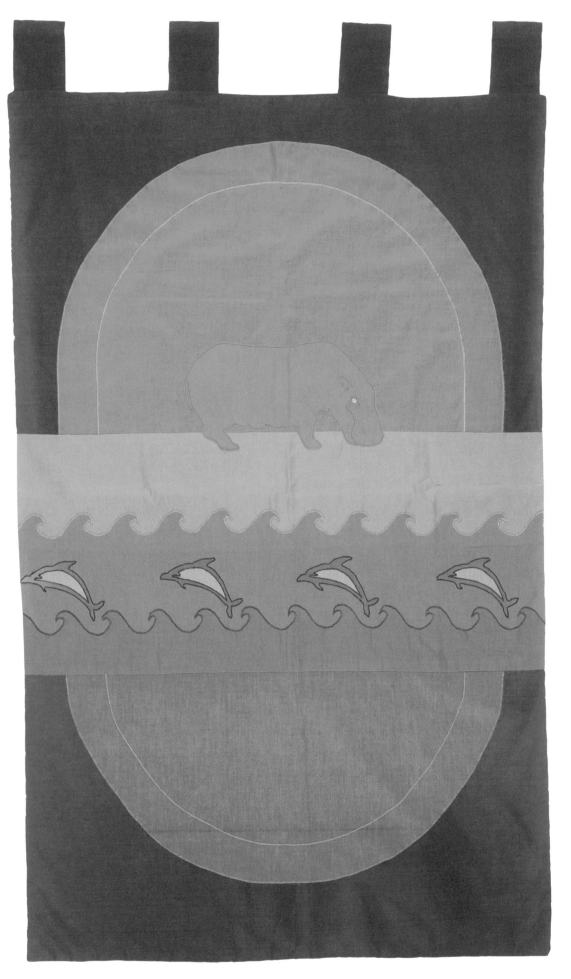

HIPPO VISITING THE BEACH, 1977
COTTON AND POLYESTER FABRIC,
56 x 36 INCHES

LITTLE GREEN STAR, 1979, COTTON AND POLYESTER FABRIC, 40 x 10 INCHES

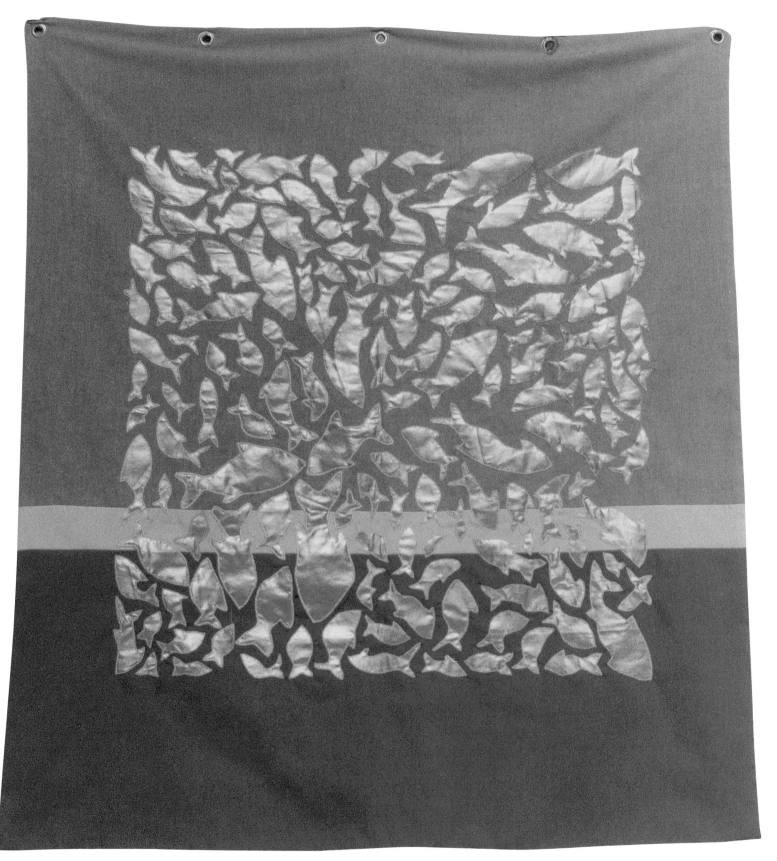

BAIT BOX, 1979, COTTON AND POLYESTER FABRIC, APPROX. 60 x 50 INCHES

BAFFLE, 1979, COTTON AND POLYESTER, THREE PANELS, 36 x 30 INCHES EACH

FIVE PIGS AT BROOM ISLAND: A PARTICULARLY FINE DAY, 1977, COTTON AND POLYESTER FABRIC, 42½ x 50½ INCHES

SILVER MOON, 1982, COTTON AND POLYESTER FABRIC, APPROX. 60 x 50 INCHES

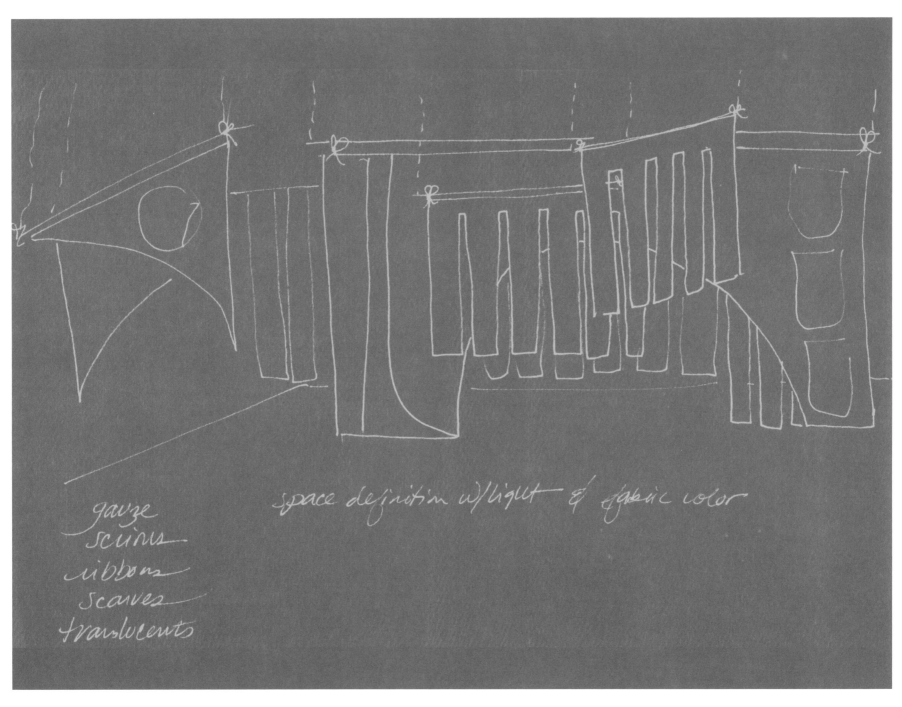

gauze
scrims
ribbons
scarves
translucents

space definition w/light & fabric color

PEN AND INK DRAWING FROM THE ARTIST'S SKETCHBOOK

GREY STRIPES, 1979, COTTON AND POLYESTER FABRIC, APPROX. 30 x 60 INCHES

UNVEILING THE *LANDMARKS* BANNER, PORTLAND, MAINE, 1979. PHOTO BY EARL STEVENS

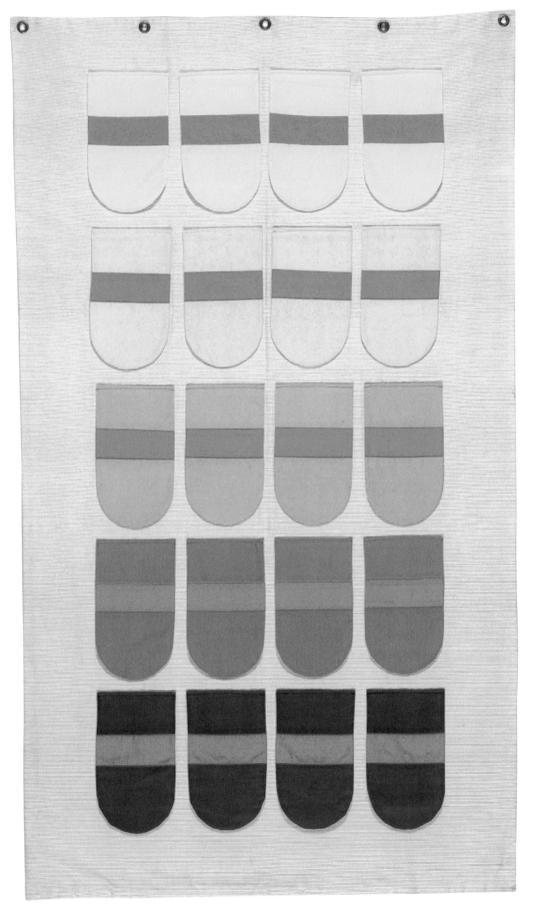

SCALES, N.D., COTTON AND POLYESTER FABRIC, 59 x 34 INCHES

ALL AMERICAN COW, 1982
COTTON AND POLYESTER FABRIC, 59½ x 24 INCHES

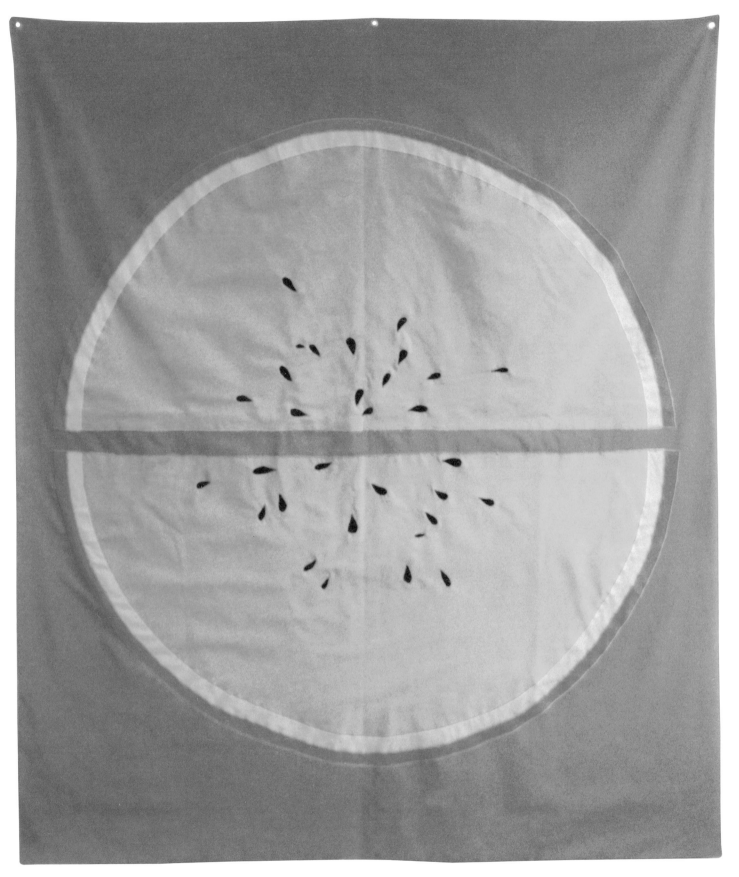

WATERMELON FLAG 2, 1978, COTTON AND POLYESTER FABRIC, APPROX. 55 x 50 INCHES

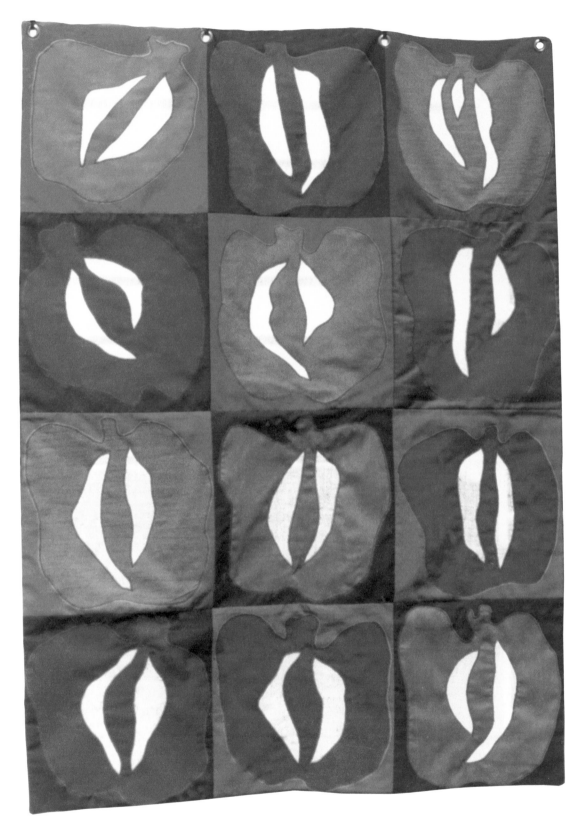

FRUIT FLAG, 1979, COTTON AND POLYESTER FABRIC, APPROX. 60 x 40 INCHES

WATERMELON FLAG, N.D., COTTON AND POLYESTER FABRIC, 20 x 24 INCHES

FRESH FISH, 1986, COTTON AND POLYESTER FABRIC, 80 x 60 INCHES

FRESH

FARMER'S MARKET, N.D.
COTTON AND POLYESTER FABRIC, 62 x 22½ INCHES

EMPEROR'S FLAG, N.D., COTTON AND POLYESTER FABRIC, 48 x 43 INCHES

MIDDLEBURY CLASS OF 1943, 1983
COTTON AND POLYESTER FABRIC,
APPROX. 56 x 35 INCHES

MIDDLEBURY CLASS OF 1973, N.D.
COTTON AND POLYESTER FABRIC,
APPROX. 56 x 35 INCHES

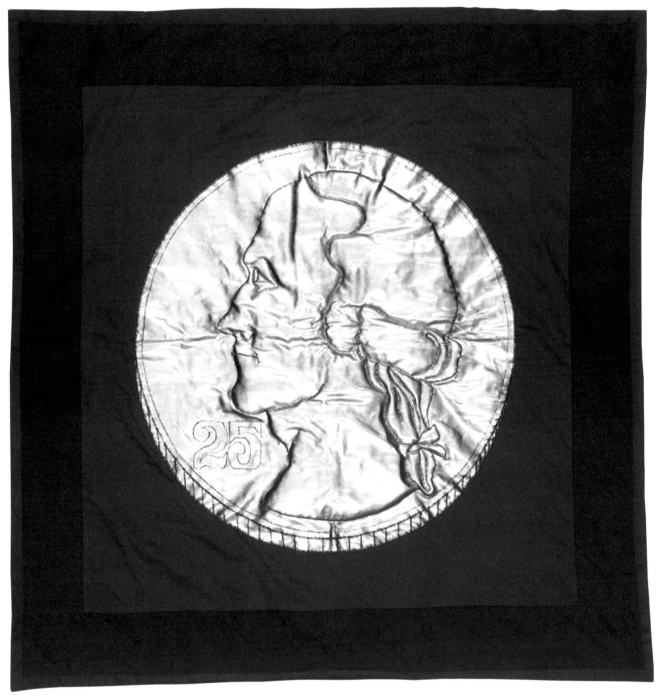

25TH ANNIVERSARY, 1979, COTTON AND POLYESTER FABRIC, 53 x 43½ INCHES

FRESHMAN RUSH, 1982, COTTON AND POLYESTER FABRIC, 114¹/₂ x 25 INCHES

CONFETTI, 1981, COTTON AND POLYESTER, 134 x 20 INCHES

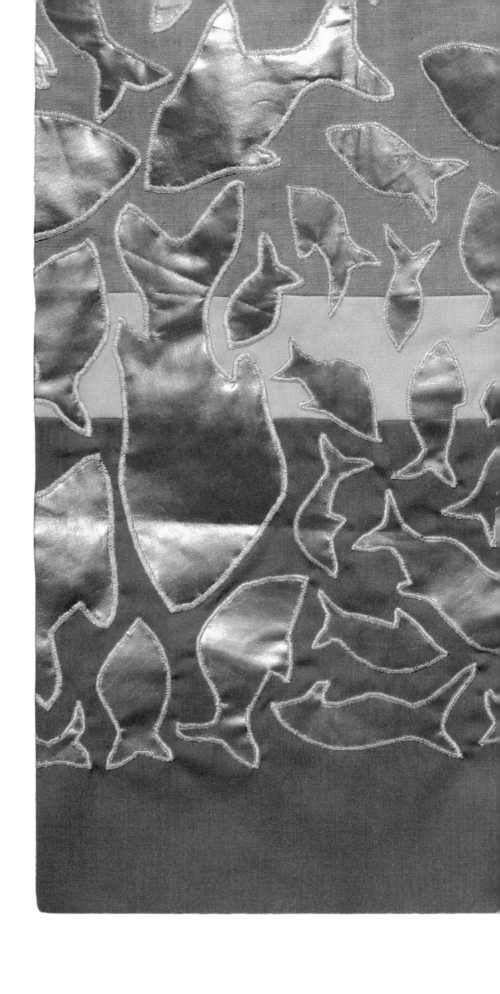

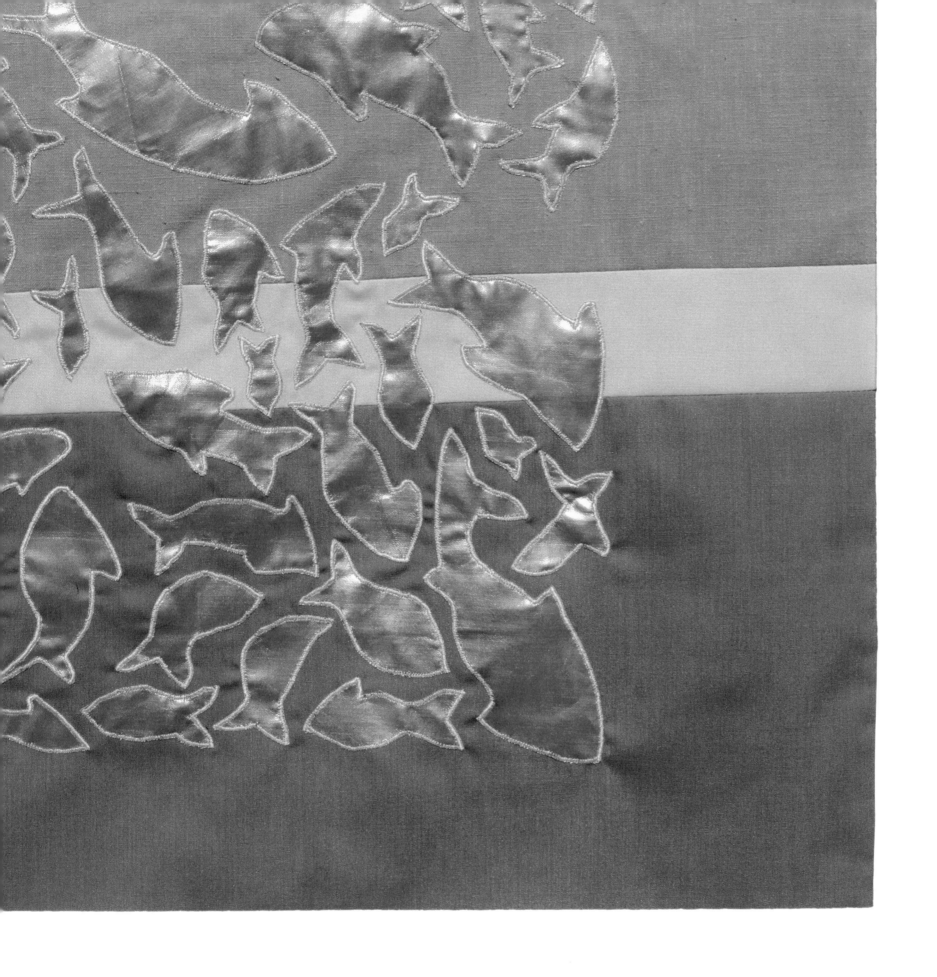

flags traditionally made
of Oxford Cotton, more
lately of Oxford Nylon

now, much ripstop nylon

———

I use ripstop, sail cloth,
cottons, blends, some
brocades, occassionally
thin vinyls (for gold &
silver), sometimes old
printed gunny sacks,
sometimes beads

PEARS, N.D., NYLON, 42 x 66½ INCHES

PREVIOUS PAGE LEFT: *SARDINE FLAG* (AT ROCKAWAY, VINALHAVEN ISLAND), N.D., NYLON, 48 x 93 INCHES
PREVIOUS PAGE RIGHT: *DEBT TO PAY* (AT ROCKAWAY, VINALHAVEN ISLAND), 1986, NYLON, 52 x 94½ INCHES

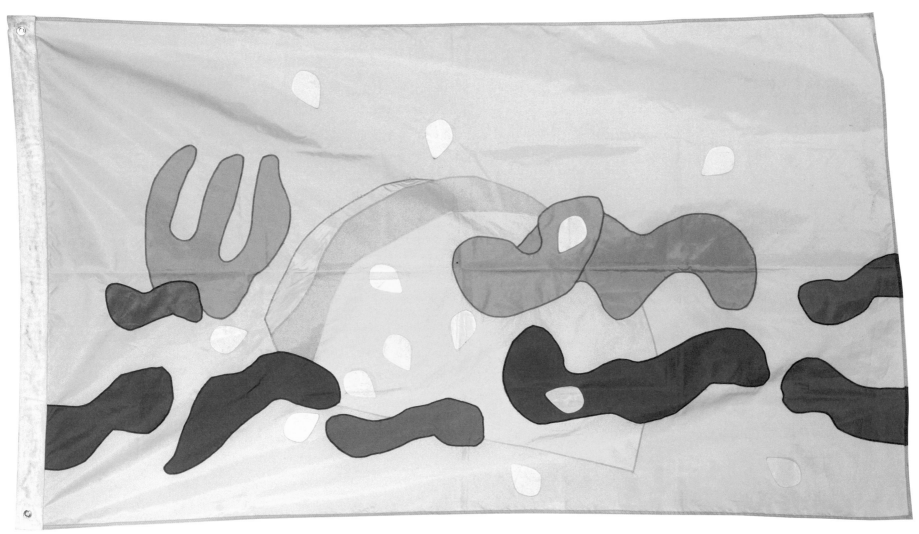

OH YOU HONEYDEW, N.D., NYLON, 48 x 87 INCHES

NIMBUS, N.D. NYLON, 57 x 76 INCHES

MAY FLAG, N.D., NYLON, 57 x 76 INCHES

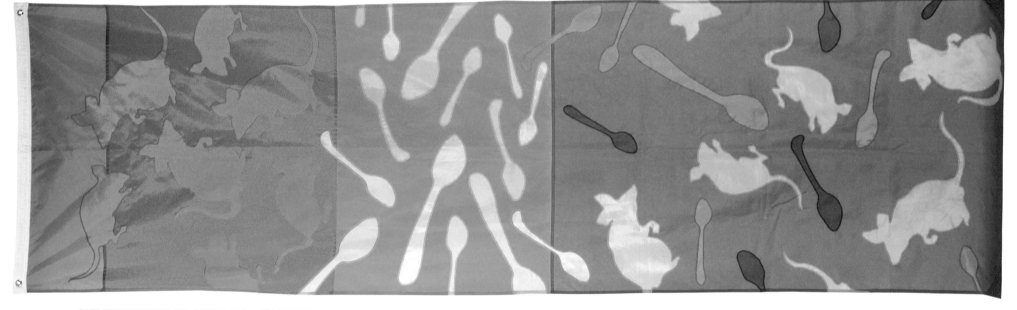

RATS IN THE PANTRY, N.D, NYLON, 126 x 35½ INCHES

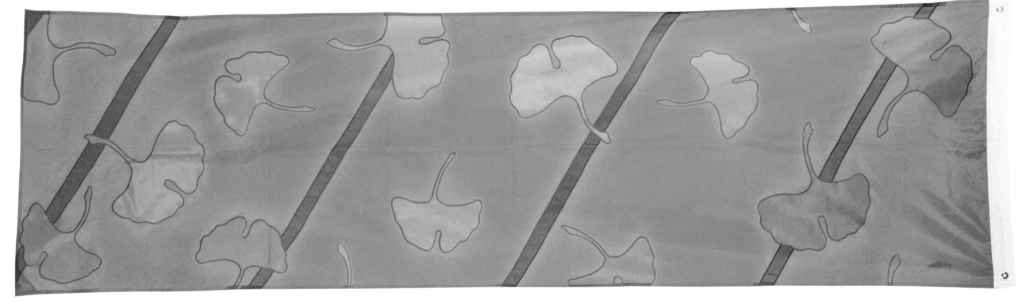

GINGKO BILOBA, N.D., NYLON FABRIC, 120 x 33 INCHES

FROM LEFT TO RIGHT: *SLICE*, N.D., NYLON, APPROX. 36 x 48 INCHES (DETAIL) | *HAPPY BIRTHDAY DEARIE*, N.D., NYLON, 48 x 84 INCHES | *STARS ABOVE, SEA BELOW*, N.D, NYLON, 48 x 84 INCHES

WEDDING FLAG, 1989, NYLON, APPROX. 36 x 48 INCHES | *HUZZA*, N.D., NYLON, 53 x 93 INCHES | *SLICE*, N.D., NYLON, APPROX. 36 x 48 INCHES (DETAIL)

UNTITLED, N.D.
NYLON FABRIC, 55 x 91 INCHES

72

DEBT TO PAY, 1986
NYLON FABRIC, 52 x 94½ INCHES

SIGNATURE FLAG, N.D., NYLON, 106 x 45½ INCHES

QUEEN WITH RED SHOES, N.D., COTTON AND POLYESTER FABRIC, APPROX. 30 x 22 INCHES

THREADS

ACCORDING TO A TRADITIONAL CHINESE proverb, invisible red threads connect us at birth to all those in the world whom we are destined to meet. It was no coincidence then that red threads—and common interests—linked Jamien and me together as art students at college in 1969. We remained close friends through regular correspondence and occasional visits between Maine and New York City until her death thirty years later.

At school, Jamien stood out right away as an exceptionally gifted draftsman. Even her handwriting danced across the page. She could draw like Rubens and carve a wood block like Dürer—her etchings and woodcuts always sold out quickly at annual student art sales. Her real love, though, was working with three-dimensional media.

Collecting and sewing with vintage fabrics became one of her favorite activities at school. We resurrected vintage cast-iron sewing machines with fancy floral stenciling and stitched together coverlets and collages from salvaged neckties. Jamien surprised one of her traditional 2-D design classes by presenting an original composition in the form of a pieced quilt. We used scraps of Victorian lace from nightcaps and antimacassars to embellish denim overalls. "Nice threads," Jamien's admirers would say as she sashayed into the dining hall upholstered in layers of antique white eyelet petticoats, a hand-knit reindeer sweater, a beaded cowboy belt, and an artistically knotted scarf on her head.

While teaching at the American School in Warsaw, Poland, after college, Jamien wrote home about her adventures and her international charges—seventy-two children from twenty-seven countries. She was delighted when some of the African students presented her with a collection of colorful batik fabrics, which they insisted she drape around herself during classes. On one occasion her flair for costumes caused a bit of a stir. At a diplomatic reception held in honor of resident Nigerians, she arrived wearing an antique blue silk Chinese robe embellished with embroideries. A group of sober Chinese nationals, dressed in regulation gray Mao suits, stared gravely as she entered. Eventually though, they invited her to their circle, complimented her robe, and explained the meaning of each embroidered vignette.

Jamien was able to keep up her artistic activities in Warsaw with a loom she installed in her rooms, and she gained access to the facilities of the Art Academy and the Polish Printmakers League through a boyfriend. During the holidays, she enjoyed excursions to Berlin, Vienna, Budapest, Spain, and Lapland. She was scheduled to start the 1975–1976 school year at a new teaching post in Beirut, but when a bloody civil war erupted there, she was forced to cancel plans and return to the United States.

After settling on Vinalhaven Island in the fall of 1975, she spent her first year patching together odd jobs for a living, including lobstering, waitressing, and farm work.

Dressed in overalls and a bandana as she drove a tractor across rocky fields, she said she felt like "a candidate for the Socialist People's Asparagus Cooperative." She was relieved to be back in a classroom when a teaching job materialized the next year on North Haven Island. While snowed in during Christmas vacation, she wrote that she had already started laying plans for the school May Day extravaganza, which would feature May pole streamers, singing, dancing, and recorder playing. "Teaching is great," she said. "It lets people like me exploit their greatest fantasies within its walls."

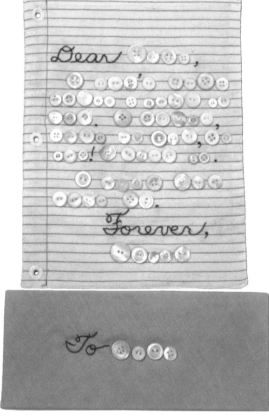

BUTTON LETTER, 1989, 8½ x 11
MIXED MEDIA, THREAD, BUTTONS ON PAPER (DETAIL)

Jamien's banners began to take shape during this time. Long familiar with the flags, pennants, and burgees that are a traditional part of seaside life, she set to creating her own spirited versions. The banners proved to be an eloquent medium for her visual genius, her natural instincts for fabric and collage, and her love of storytelling, whimsy, and humor.

Christening her business "Liberty Banners," Jamien limned a trade card with the image of a turreted castle waving flags from each peak. The playful legend advertises "CUSTOM DESIGNED flags, banners, pennants, vexilla, semaphors, jacks, standards, streamers, drapeaux, oriflamb, ensigns, labara, gonfalons, burgees, bunting, pavillions FOR celebrations, weddings, long lost friends, tree houses, birthdays, blank walls, favorite aunts, new babies, sports events, bountiful gardens, successful businesses, new homes & grey days."

Some of the Liberty Banners designs were dictated by special orders, but Jamien preferred to let her own imagination set the course. She sometimes felt that commissions allowed "too little artistic leeway." The banner sizes ranged widely, from small pennants designed to be clustered together to huge architectural pieces like the *Landmarks* panel (1979) that hung from the exterior of the Hay Building in Portland, Maine, in the manner of a giant Polish propaganda banner.

Island landscapes figured prominently in the earliest Liberty Banners, as in *Stars Above, Stars Below* (1978), with its bands of water, forest, sunburst, and stars. Pigs were also frequent motifs, perhaps recalling those she had photographed in Polish farmyards. The *Blue Pig 1A* (circa 1978) has

a zipper sewn in along his flank, revealing a witty peek at a USDA label just inside. The *Close Enough* banner (1976), featuring a bright blue boar, is named for a cabin where Jamien once camped out and where friends gather annually for a reunion. She gave this pig a slightly wary stance, perhaps to indicate his growing concern with preparations at an adjacent roasting pit.

In 1979 Jamien shifted her focus from "piggies and pine trees" to more abstract compositions with intense color combinations. She made a number of hangings with geometric patterns in supersaturated hues that she likened to Amish quilts. Among the most striking of her banners are a number featuring watermelons composed of simple circles and wedges cut from vibrant cerise, persimmon, and chartreuse fabrics. These bring to mind the colors and shapes of traditional Polish paper cutouts and lacquer ware.

A marine animal theme threads its way through Jamien's banners. An early panel features a well-articulated green fish bursting from wriggling splashes of blue water. In the *Bait Box* hanging (1979), abstracted fish forms cut from reflective fabric create a shimmering pool of light and motion. Jamien showed the banners *Catfish Comics* (1982) and *Large Cod with Silver Speckles* (1979) (images not available) at a group exhibition of Fish Art and Musical Performances in New York City in 1982. For opening night, the chamber music group Chelsea Ensemble played Franz Schubert's "Trout Quintet."

By the early 1980s, Jamien spoke of her determination to be a "serious banner maker" and felt she was beginning to find her own style. Making time for the banners became more of a challenge however as her family grew and later when illness struck. Other creative ventures also diverted her attention from the banners; among them were Flea Circus Hats featuring apparel that she had constructed from "recycled & reclaimed fabrics, antique buttons, bits & pieces, heart & soul & humor." During her last years, she experimented with paper collage, musing that she had become "a cut-and-paste idiot," but admitting that she had "discovered an amazing & wonderful peace in the studio."

In her personal life, Jamien was very much a flag bearer. Throughout her years she spoke out for environmental concerns, education, world peace, and other causes to which she was committed. Living with cancer forced her to be even more of a warrior. Like others before her, she took comfort by going into battle holding her colors high.

Deborah Sampson Shinn

On the occasion of the 14th Anniversary
of the Independence
of the Federal Republic of Nigeria
the Charge d'Affaires, Mr. Phil. Ogwuazor

has the honour to invite

Miss Morehouse

to a reception at the Diplomatic Club,
Jablonna on October 1, 1974 at 18.00–20.00

R.S.V.P. 17-50-83
(Regrets Only)

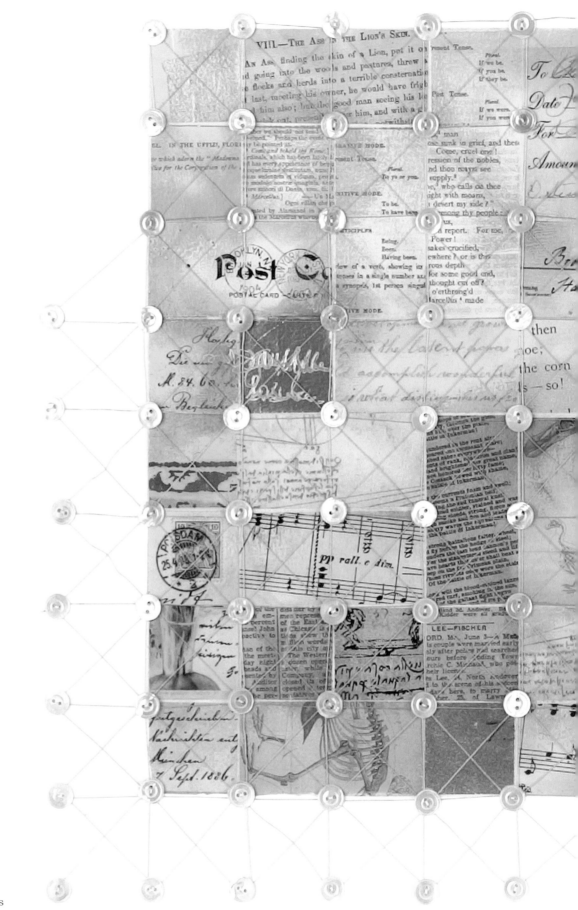

UNTITLED, 1996, MIXED MEDIA, THREAD, STAMPS, BUTTONS ON PAPER, 22 x 30 INCHES

FISH, N.D.
COTTON AND POLYESTER FABRIC,
APPROX. 30 x 20 INCHES

FRESH FISH
by Jamien Morehouse

FRESH FISH
by Jamien Morehouse

83

FRESH FISH
by James Meadowre

ACKNOWLEDGMENTS

THE FARNSWORTH ART MUSEUM'S FORMAL connection to Jamien Morehouse (1951–1999) dates to the summer of 2000, and the opening of the Jamien Morehouse Wing. The inaugural exhibition was titled *On Island: A Century of Continuity and Change* and celebrated the islands of the Maine archipelago as seen through the eyes of some of the country's most notable artists. It was a subject close to island-dweller Jamien's heart and entirely appropriate to her memory.

With this book and exhibition, the Farnsworth once again honors Jamien Morehouse—this time as an artist in her own right. She takes her place with other artists who have distinguished the state of Maine with their talent and creative energy. Like so many others, she found inspiration in the natural beauty of the state and responded with her own unique vision. Through this publication and exhibition we celebrate her art, her enduring spirit and her love of Maine.

Our most sincere thanks are due to Charles and Julie Cawley and the Cawley Family Foundation, whose generous contribution and committed support made both the exhibition and this publication possible. Mr. Cawley's accomplice in this process has been Samuel Conkling, Jamien's son, who contributed invaluable insight to his mother's art. Sam and Victoria K. Woodhull have led the book to completion, tracked down lost works, photography, and related material, and provided the groundwork on which the show has been built. In so doing they have created a valuable archive that greatly enriches our understanding of Jamien's life and work.

Other members of the Conkling family also provided immeasurable assistance. The Museum thanks Philip, Tim, James and Micah Conkling, Jamien's parents Dick and Lee Morehouse, and her brother Bruce Morehouse for their cooperation in loaning the majority of the banners and other works by Jamien included in the exhibition, and for supporting the concept of the project from its inception. The Conkling and Morehouse family collections of Jamien's work have been enhanced by the addition of loans from other lenders. To all those who shared their treasured works with the museum audience, we extend our thanks.

For their illuminating essays we thank Christopher B. Crosman, Samuel Conkling, Victoria K. Woodhull and Deborah Shinn. Their words bring Jamien Morehouse the artist into clear focus and establish the first comprehensive survey of her work. The book provides a structure on which future scholarship can be built.

We also thank Harrah Lord of Yellow House Studio for her collaboration with this handsome book and design of the related exhibition and programming materials. Once again,

her impeccable sense of the visual has produced striking results. Copy editor Elizabeth IlgenFritz proficiently shaped the words in this book into a fluid whole, and we thank her for her meticulous efforts. We are grateful to photographer Earl Stevens for permission to use his wonderful images of Jamien and her work. Thanks also to Amy Wilton, Ron Simons and Rick Echlemeyer who provided new photography of many of the banners that appear in this book, Peter and Sandy Koons for publication assistance, and to Mary Politowsky and Jake Dowling who provided valuable assistance in the early stages of research.

Our thanks to all the members of the Farnsworth Museum staff, for their stellar efforts and generous cooperation. Chief Curator, Suzette McAvoy, contributed administrative oversight of the project and kept us all on track. Melissa Olson, Director of Education, David Stucky, Director of Marketing, and their respective staff, Angela Waldron, Registrar, Betsy Jewell, Curatorial Assistant and Jo Hluska, Preparator, all worked in concert to make the exhibition both meaningful and memorable.

Finally and most importantly, we recognize and honor Jamien Morehouse for creating these bright and joyful banners worked so lovingly with her accomplished hands. They reveal a keen appreciation for the comedic, the fantastic and

the time-honored rituals of everyday life. They also tell of a life spent in gladness and giving. Through her art we appreciate her boundless creativity and humor, her honoring of home, friends and family, and her love of the natural environment. Her soul lives on in these wonderful creations. In a sense, this book and the exhibition *Jamien Morehouse: Liberty Banners* is a gift to the community, one that carries her spirit out into time and space.

Helen Ashton Fisher
Curator of Exhibitions
Farnsworth Art Museum

PIG BURGEE, N.D., COTTON, 14 x 20 INCHES
HAND PENNANTS, N.D., NYLON, APPROX. 12 x 12 INCHES

87

THANKS

I WAS IN ITALY EIGHT MONTHS AGO when the conception for this project came up in a telephone conversation with the States, and the band of people to whom I owe thanks literally stretches that distance of the Atlantic.

On getting back to Maine from the semester abroad, I wrote a letter on the boat out to Vinalhaven and sent copies of it off to a list of names I pulled from my mom's address book. I got great response from a number of people that I hadn't seen in a long time, and some I'd never met. I spoke early on to a Professor of hers from Middlebury, David Bumbeck, who remembered her print work from his classes in the early seventies. I also heard from Deborah Shinn at the beginning of that summer, another Middlebury student, a good friend of my mom's. Working with Deborah was a great thing. Word of mouth connections pulled Victoria Woodhull and me along and across the Thorofare to North Haven, where Barney Hallowell and Herb Parsons provided more early support—from Barney, memories of my mom's philosophy as a teacher, and from Herb, a veritable collection of commissioned work as well as sales records from his years as her dealer on the island. Kelly

Richards and Frances Ditzler, back on Vinalhaven, also had recollections of her island life and beyond. On the mainland, Kalla Bucholtz, another fellow artist and friend, remembered the quirky details vividly, and rounded out a perception of my mother that I tried to write into my essay. June LaCombe was another early source I'm glad to have spoken with in this way. As I mentioned in the opening of the book, the lives of these banners are interesting things in themselves, and are told differently by each of the lenders, many of whom let me into their houses and barns and sheds where these works hang. I owe gratitude to these people.

My father, of course, was another invaluable resource, both in the way of his wide memory, which worked with great specificity back to my mother's Portland years, as well as his skill as an editor, and ability to help me shape my bit of writing. To all early readers of early drafts and those with enthusiastic support for this whole production—my brothers, friends, Shannon, Laura, Daniel Stupar, Gitti, my thanks.

Next, I must say that through and through, I've been hugely lucky to work beside Victoria

Woodhull who has tolerated me up to exactly the right point, and provided great direction all along. She also came along with a toolbox of essential connections to the professional crew who helped write, edit (Elizabeth IlgenFritz), design (Helen Fisher), frame (Stan Klein) and bring together a successful show and publication. (I write this knowing it will be.) With Harrah Lord, another key creative mind in the mix, we had many an animated conversation, and never came to blows. Thanks also to Dock, for surrendering some of his usual attention.

Here, I'd like to acknowledge one more truly essential part of this production, Charlie Cawley, a great friend of mine. His support has been genuine and constant since we met some seven years ago.

Finally, I write a line for my Grandparents, Dick and Lee Morehouse, whose blessing on the project has been articulated through a continual support that I'm fortunate to have and sense in a strong way. They are, of course, the groundwork for the whole story.

Ok.

Sam.

February 2006

GOOD WOODEN BOATS FROM MAINE, CIRCA 1983, COTTON AND POLYESTER FABRIC, 30 x 120 INCHES

LENDERS

We would like to gratefully acknowledge
the following lenders to the exhibition
at the Farnsworth Art Museum
March 19–June 18, 2006

Close Enough, Bragg Hill, Vermont
Mary and Thomas Amory
Peter and Kelly Richards
Annie and Perry Boyden
Marnie and Peter Frost
Middlebury College
David M. Parsons
June C. Hopkins
Frank Simon
Jan B. Taft
Lydia Sparrow
June LaCombe
Thom Buescher
Jane McLaughlin
Bruce Morehouse &
Christine Anderson Morehouse
Dick & Lee Morehouse
Two private collections
Conkling/Morehouse Family

STARS ABOVE, STARS BELOW, 1978, COTTON AND POLYESTER FABRIC, APPROX. 60 x 12 INCHES

Jamien Morehouse (1951–1999)

1951

Born in Lexington, Massachusetts

1952–2006

Morehouse family summers on Vinalhaven
   Island, Maine

1969–1973

Middlebury College—B.A., Fine Arts

1973–1975

Teaches at the America School in Warsaw, Poland,
   and travels to Berlin, Vienna, Budapest, Spain,
   and Lapland

1975

Establishes Liberty Banners

1976

Creates first banner, *Fifth Annual Festival of Life,
   Close Enough, Vermont*

1976–1978

Teaches kindergarten on North Haven Island and
   lives on Vinalhaven Island

1978

Creates *Landmarks* Banner

1978–1980

Serves as the Director of the Children's Resource
   Center in Portland, Maine

1979

Researches and writes environmental education
   curriculum for the Maine Audubon Society

1980

Marries Philip Conkling, a forester, who would
found the Island Institute in 1983

1980

Begins new line of work with nylon fabric

1981

Director of Maine Teachers Center in Rockport,
Maine

1981–1982

Works in the Environmental Education Depart-
ment of the Office of Energy Resources in
Augusta, Maine

1982

Son Tim, born

1983, 1984

Participates in fiber arts shows at the Hopkins
Gallery, North Haven Island, Maine

1983–1987

Establishes and co-manages *Fizgigs*, a children's
knitwear company, based in Belfast, Maine

1984

Son Sam, born

1984

Moves to Rockport, Maine

1985–1988

Helps establish and participate in *Common
Threads*, a monthly fiber arts collaborative

1986

Holds first banner-making workshop with College
of the Atlantic, Bar Harbor, Maine

1986

Exhibits banners at Calderwood Hall, North Haven
Island, Maine

1987

Exhibition of *Island Garden Series.* Group show
with Eric Hopkins and Michelle O'Keefe, Tarra-
tine Club, Bangor, Maine

1988

Sons Micah and James, born

Continues work with College of the Atlantic,
Bar Harbor, Maine

1988

Bangor Seminary commissions

1989

Flags sold in Antarctica—aboard ship for
  Antarctica Society Expeditions
Begins fish paintings and burgees

1989–1993

Edits newspaper column "Waste Watch" for the
  Camden Herald

1992

Develops "fresh fish" distinct label
Begins making hats

1992–1999

Establishes and helps manage an annual
  Christmas "Hat Show" as a benefit for
  New Hope for Women

1993

Begins wooden snake series
Exhibits work at Holly Hill Galleries,
  Wiscasset, Maine

1994

Creates Farnsworth Art Museum banners for
  opening the Nevelson Gallery

1994

Travels to Moscow and St. Petersburg

1995

As resident artist, teaches and oversees Camden
  Youth Arts sewing and fiber arts residency for
  girls at risk program

1996

Establishes "Pies for Peace" to supply Russian
  factory fishing ship in Penobscot Bay, Maine,
  with 50 locally baked pies

1996

Travels to Moscow, boards Trans-Siberian
  Railroad to Novosibirsk, returns via the Central
  Asian Republics of Kazakhstan, Uzbekistan
  and Georgia

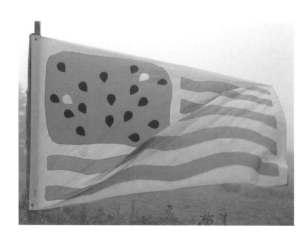

LIBERTY MELON, N.D., NYLON, 49 x 78 INCHES

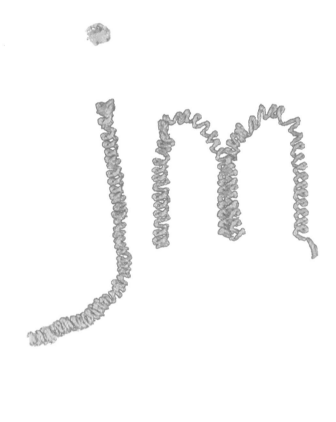